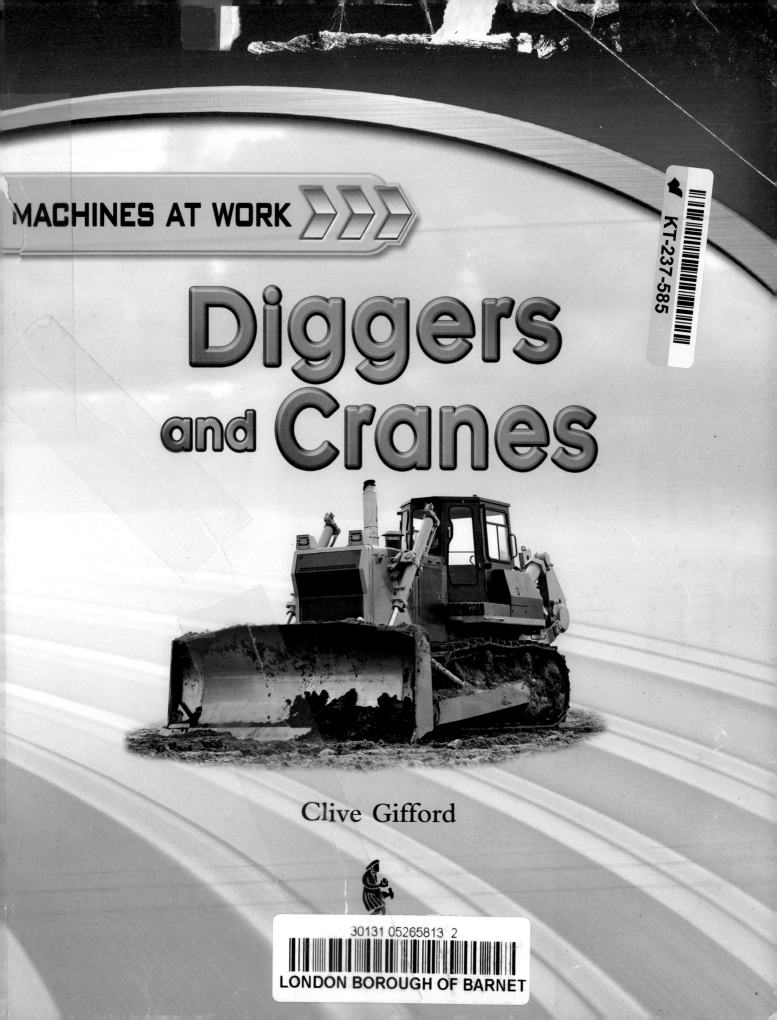

MACHINES AT WORK >>>

Diggers and Cranes

Clive Gifford

Published in 2013 by Wayland
Copyright © Wayland 2013

Wayland
338 Euston Road
London NW1 3BH

Wayland Australia
Level 17/207 Kent Street
Sydney, NSW 2000

Editor: Nicola Edwards
Designer: Elaine Wilkinson
Picture Researcher: Clive Gifford

British Library Cataloguing in Publication
Data

Gifford, Clive.
    Diggers and cranes. --
    (Machines at work)
    1. Excavating machinery--Juvenile
    literature. 2. Cranes,
    derricks, etc.--Juvenile literature.
    I. Title II. Series
    629.2'25-dc23

ISBN: 978 0 7502 7807 2

10 9 8 7 6 5 4 3 2 1

Printed in China

Wayland is a division of Hachette Children's
Books, an Hachette UK company
www.hachette.co.uk

To find out about the author, visit his website:
www.clivegifford.co.uk

Picture acknowledgements:
The author and publisher would like to thank
the following agencies and people for allowing
these pictures to be reproduced:
Cover (main) ssuaphotos / Shutterstock.
com, (inset) Balazs Toth / Shutterstock.
com; title page Steve Mann / Shutterstock.
com, p3 Sascha Hahn / Shutterstock.com;
p4 (t) Christopher Parypa / Shutterstock.
com, (b) Robert Crum / Shutterstock.
com; p5 Natali Glado / Shutterstock.com;
p6 Pablo Scapinachis / Shutterstock.com;
p7 (t) Robert Rozbora / Shutterstock.com,
(b) karamysh / Shutterstock.com; p8 Sascha
Hahn / Shutterstock.com; p9 (t) Eugene
Berman / Shutterstock.com, (b) Khafizov
Ivan Harisovich / Shutterstock.com; p10 (l)
David Acosta Allely / Shutterstock.com, (r)
courtesy of AgustaWestland; p11 jakelv7500
/ Shutterstock.com; p12 Carlos E. Santa
Maria / Shutterstock.com; p13 (t) iStock
© Simon Parker, (b) Michael G Smith /
Shutterstock.com; p14 (l) Maurizio Milanesio
/ Shutterstock.com, (r) David Fowler /
Shutterstock.com; p15 dvande / Shutterstock.
com; p16 Steve Mann / Shutterstock.
com; p17 (t) Louise Cukrov / Shutterstock.
com, (b) R McIntyre / Shutterstock.com;
p18 Andrej Poi / Shutterstock.com; p19 (t)
Maria Hetting / Shutterstock.com, (b) Steve
Mann / Shutterstock.com; p20 iStock © Eric
Gevaert; p21 (t) Remzi / Shutterstock.com
(b) Losevsky Pavel / Shutterstock.com; p23
iStock © Anna Ivanova; p24 Balazs Toth /
Shutterstock.com

Contents

Diggers and cranes at work	4
Clearing the ground	6
Digging deep	8
Different diggers	10
Mining and tunnelling	12
Cranes on the move	14
Container cranes	16
Tower cranes	18
Demolition!	20
Quiz	22
Glossary	23
Index	24

Diggers and cranes at work

Cranes and diggers are big machines that move heavy loads. Diggers work on building sites, in mines and on farms. Cranes lift and move loads on building sites, at docks, on oil rigs and on roads.

Two diggers gather and move broken bits of brick and stone at a building site in China. In the background a giant tower crane is being used to help construct a new building.

Tower crane lifts loads up high

Driver sits and controls digger from here

Arm of digger stretches outwards

Metal bucket scoops up rock and stone

Many diggers and cranes run on caterpillar tracks. These help the vehicle go over bumps more smoothly than wheels and stop the machine sinking into soft, muddy ground.

Sitting in the cab, the crane driver controls the levers that raise and lower the crane arm to move the load.

Cranes and diggers are operated by a driver, who sits inside part of the machine called a cab. Controls in the cab move the different parts of the crane or digger.

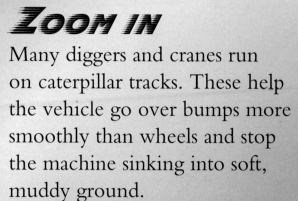

FAST FACT

Most diggers on building sites are yellow because scientists have found that yellow is the easiest colour to see there.

Clearing the ground

Bulldozers are used in places such as building sites where large areas of ground need to be cleared. At the front of a bulldozer is a giant steel blade. The blade can push away large amounts of dirt, rubble, sand or snow to clear an area.

Gases from the engine leave the bulldozer from this pipe

Arms move the blade up or down

ZOOM IN

A ripper is a sharp claw fitted to the back of some bulldozers. It is often used to tear up hard ground in preparation for laying pipes.

Bulldozers can help level beaches and clear them of extra sand thrown up by the sea during a storm

A bulldozer scoops up earth in its blade to clear an area of ground.

When a bulldozer's blade is lifted it scoops up its load and carries it upwards. When the blade is lowered its sharp bottom edge cuts into the earth and pushes it away. This helps it level an area of ground.

Track made of metal links grips the ground

Digging deep

Backhoe excavators are a type of digger. They are used for lots of jobs, from demolition and ditch digging to making holes for building foundations or trenches for carrying pipes.

A backhoe excavator has a powerful arm on the end of which is a metal bucket. The bucket can be tilted back and forth to dig into and scoop up earth or rubble. The digger's long arm can reach down a long way to dig deep holes or trenches.

Top half of the digger turns while the base stays still

Part of the arm called the boom can be raised or lowered

Bucket tilts forward then moves back to dig into earth

Engine in rear of excavator

An excavator dumps its load of sand into a dumper truck. Once the truck is full, it will carry the load away.

The top half of most excavators can turn while the base on its tracks stays in position. This allows the excavator to dig in one place and then turn to drop the earth elsewhere.

FAST FACT

If all the backhoe diggers made in a year by the JCB company worked together, they could move 1.3 billion tonnes of earth.

ZOOM IN

The bucket of a backhoe excavator is usually made of steel. Its sharp metal prongs, or teeth, cut into the earth with ease.

Different diggers

There are many types of digger. These range in size from giant machines used in mines and on building sites to tiny excavators used in gardens or small streets.

FAST FACT

Big Muskie was the world's biggest excavator used for coal mining. Its giant bucket could hold two buses side by side.

Loader bucket tilts up and down to scoop up or drop its load

Driver controls loader from the cab

This bucket loader has four wheels covered in rubber tyres. The giant scoop at the front can dig and carry large amounts of earth and other material.

Chunky tyre pattern helps digger to grip the ground

ZOOM IN

This metal rod, called a hydraulic piston, moves the excavator's arm. The piston is pushed back and forth by liquid in a cylinder. It moves with great force, helping the excavator dig into hard ground and lift heavy loads.

Some mini excavators are small enough to fit through the front door of a house. They work well in cramped places such as gardens, at roadworks and inside old buildings.

A mini excavator works on breaking up the ground so that pipes can be laid under a new road.

Mining and tunnelling

Some of the biggest diggers of all are used to mine coal and other materials or to carve out giant tunnels underground. These machines have to move huge amounts of rock and earth every day.

Each bucket is large enough to hold a car

Cables lower the wheel until its buckets dig into the ground

Giant boom with bucket wheel on the end

This bucket wheel excavator has more than a dozen buckets all fitted to a giant wheel that turns with great force. Each bucket scrapes away at the ground, digging up coal that lies on or just under the surface.

Many diggers and mining machines work underground to mine rich seams of coal, gold or other valuable materials. Other underground machines bore large, long holes which will become road or underground train tunnels.

ZOOM IN

The cutting head of a tunnel boring machine is circular and covered with sharp metal teeth and cutting rollers which cut through underground rock.

A tunnel boring machine is checked before it begins work. It will be helping to bore a large tunnel for an underground train system in Poland.

Cranes on the move

Cranes lift loads up and move them around. Some cranes are fixed in place, but many can move. These include cranes on breakdown trucks, fire engines and on some boats and ships.

Crane arm

The arm of this mobile crane is made of different parts that fit inside each other. They can slide out to extend the crane arm so that it can reach up higher.

Supports called outriggers stick out from the side of the crane

Cranes can come to the rescue, picking up heavy objects that have fallen or lifting overturned vehicles. This crane picks up a boat washed onto land after a heavy storm struck the island of Ibiza.

Crane hook attaches to load

A crane lifts up loads attached to its large hook. The hook is connected to a long cable. The other end of the cable is wound round a cylinder called a winch. An electric motor turns the winch to raise or lower the hook.

ZOOM IN

Some cranes use a giant magnet instead of a hook to lift up iron and steel in a scrapyard.

Container cranes

Containers are large metal boxes that can hold all sorts of cargo, from tools to toys. All containers are the same size. This allows them to be loaded and then transported more easily by ships at sea and trucks on land. Container cranes are mostly found at docks and ports.

A container crane works at a port loading and unloading ships. A full 6m-long container can weigh up to 30,000kg. Some cranes can handle more than 25 containers per hour.

A container is lifted straight upwards by a crane. A trolley then moves it along the arm of the crane. The container is lowered onto the dock or directly onto the back of a truck to be driven away.

ZOOM IN

This is a device called a spreader. It is lowered from the crane onto the top of a container where it locks into place. The container can then be lifted up high by the crane.

A crane called a straddle carrier drives along on wheels. It picks up containers on the dock and stacks them all together.

Tower cranes

Tower cranes are the biggest cranes around. They are made up of a large metal tower with a long arm called a boom or jib on top. These cranes lift the materials that are used to build tall structures such as city skyscrapers.

Arm of crane supported by metal cables

Tower made of strong metal frame

A tall crane towers over skyscrapers in Hong Kong. It lifts a large steel girder that will form part of the frame of a building.

FAST FACT

The Kroll K-10000 is one of the world's biggest tower cranes. It is over 120m tall and it can lift a 40-tonne load.

A lifting hook runs along this crane's arm on a wheeled trolley. The crane driver controls the trolley, reeling it in towards the cab or moving it outwards to the far end of the arm.

ZOOM IN

Heavy concrete slabs are fitted to the short end of a crane's arm. They balance the load the crane is lifting. Without them, the crane might topple over.

Demolition!

Diggers and cranes are used to help construct buildings but they can also be used to tear them down – a job called demolition. Working together, these machines can reduce a building to rubble in hours.

A crane swings a heavy steel wrecking ball to knock part of a wall down. Water is used to reduce the amount of dust caused by the demolition.

Worker pumps water through hose

Wrecking ball smashes through wall of building

The bucket on an excavator can be removed and replaced with other tools that are useful for tearing buildings apart. These include powerful drills that can break up stone, and concrete crushers.

ZOOM IN

This fearsome set of metal jaws belong to a concrete crusher. The jaws tear and rip with great force.

This excavator is using its metal bucket to tear down walls of a building. Loader excavators and bulldozers will then clear the rubble away.

Quiz

So how much do you know about diggers and cranes at work? Try this quick quiz to find out!

1. What sort of machine pushes earth and other material around with a large metal blade?
a) excavator
b) bulldozer
c) tower crane

2. What are the tracks on diggers and cranes called?
a) caterpillar tracks
b) chrysalis tracks
c) butterfly tracks

3. What object moves along the arm of a crane carrying a load below it?
a) the cab
b) the jib
c) the trolley

4. What can a shipping container carried by a crane weigh when full?
a) 100kg
b) 2,400kg
c) 30,000kg

5. What item is fitted to some bulldozers to tear up hard ground?
a) a wrecking ball
b) a ripper
c) a cutting head

6. What are hydraulic pistons moved by?
a) compressed air
b) electricity
c) liquids in cylinders

7. What is one the world's biggest tower cranes called?
a) Kroll K-10000
b) Bagger 293
c) Komatsu D575A

8. What is a concrete crusher used for?
a) digging trenches
b) demolition work
c) rescuing broken-down vehicles

Glossary

bucket the scoop-like container on the end of a digger's arm

cab the part of a digger or crane where the driver sits and operates the vehicle's controls

caterpillar tracks wide belts made of metal or rubber which turn to move some diggers or cranes

concrete a heavy, solid building material made from sand, cement, water and stone

demolition the controlled destruction and dismantling of a building or other structure such as a bridge

engine the part of a vehicle which generates power to turn its wheels or tracks

foundations the parts of the building, usually below ground, that support the rest of the structure

load the material carried by diggers and cranes

outriggers bars which stick out from the side of a crane and support it while it lifts

rubble chunks of rock, brick, stone and other materials found at building and demolition sites

skyscraper a very tall building, often a hotel, apartment or office block in a city

tonne a measure of weight equal to 1,000kg

tower crane a tall crane made of metal frames that is used to build skyscrapers

tread the pattern of grooves on the surface of a tyre

Further Information

Books

On The Go: Diggers David and Penny Glover, Wayland, 2011

Machines Rule! On The Building Site Steve Parker, Franklin Watts, 2011

Machines On The Move: Diggers Andrew Langley, Franklin Watts, 2010

Big Machines: Bulldozers David and Penny Glover, Franklin Watts, 2008

Websites

http://www.jcbexplore.com/content/about_jcb/
A fun website with facts and games produced by digger makers JCB.

http://www.deckrane.com/info/towercrn.pdf
A guide to how giant tower cranes are built and work.

http://www.bigtrucksforkids.com
This website has photographs and videos of bulldozers, diggers and dump trucks.

Places to Visit

Diggerland
http://www.diggerland.com/
Not just one but four different theme parks based on diggers, cranes and dumper trucks, found in Devon, Durham, Kent and Yorkshire in the UK.

Index

arm 4, 5, 6, 8, 11, 14, 17, 18, 19

balance 19

blade 6, 7

boom 8, 12, 18

bucket 8, 10, 12, 21

building sites 4, 6, 10

bulldozers 6, 7

cab 5 10, 19

cable 15

caterpillar tracks 5, 7

claw 7

clearing ground 6, 7

concrete crusher 21

containers 16, 17

controls 5

cutting head 13

demolition 8, 20, 21

ditch digging 8

docks 4, 16, 17

driver 4, 5, 10, 19

engine 8

excavators 8, 9, 10, 11, 21

farms 4

foundations 8

gardens 10, 11

hook 15, 19

hydraulic piston 11

lifting 7, 10, 14, 15, 17, 18, 19

load 4, 5, 7, 9, 10, 15, 19

magnet 15

mines 4, 10, 12, 13

mobile cranes 14, 15

oil rigs 4

outriggers 14

pipes 6, 8, 11

ripper 7

roadworks 11

spreader 17

straddle carrier 17

tearing 7, 21

tower cranes 4, 18, 19

trenches 8

trolley 17, 19

tunnelling 12, 13

tyres 10

wheels 5, 10

wrecking ball 20